Who Said Women Can't Preach?

by

Apostle Alton R. Williams

Understanding For Life Ministries

Collierville, Tennessee

Who Said Women Can't Preach?
ISBN 0-9721504-0-4
Copyright © 2002 by
Apostle Alton R. Williams

Published by
Understanding For Life Ministries
P. O. Box 1481
Collierville, Tennessee 38027-1481

2002
First Edition

Contents

Foreword

God called me to the ministry in August 1994. I remember feeling a little apprehensive, no, *extremely* apprehensive because my mother was a preacher and I witnessed firsthand the persecution she endured. (And this was long before it became popular for women to go public with their calling.)

I thank God for having a loving, supportive husband who understands the importance of "divine destiny." He has never denied or tried to suppress my calling, but instead, he has helped to nurture it. Because he accepted my calling, I have been free to move in the gifts that God has placed inside of me.

Apostle Alton R. Williams has received a divine revelation from God concerning "women in ministry." At World Overcomers Outreach Ministries Church, where he serves as Senior Pastor, women are free to operate in their gifts and callings. They have been released to teach, preach, lead corporate prayer, lay hands on the sick, prophesy, counsel others, minister to those in need, and fulfill their God-given assignments.

The Word of God says, *"And ye shall know the truth, and the truth shall make you free"* (John 8:32). The life-changing book that you are holding in your hands will liberate your thinking concerning women in ministry and other female-centered issues in the church.

For many years, there have been erroneous beliefs concerning women, mainly because there was a lack of knowledge among believers. I grew up in a strict Pentecostal Holiness church where I noticed traditional beliefs were being passed down through the generations. We were taught that it was a sin to wear slacks, makeup, or excessive jewelry. When a woman dressed in this manner, she was accused of having a "Jezebel spirit." There was also a long list of religious rules that we had to obey if we wanted to stay sanctified. We were taught that violating these rules would cause us to backslide and would be displeasing to God, which meant we would experience His wrath and judgment. So many of us ended up running in intense fear to the altar to repent *every Sunday* and begging God to save us *again* so we wouldn't go to hell.

Thank God I am *free* today! I'm no longer a prisoner of my own beliefs that were incorrectly taught due to mis-interpretation of the Scriptures. It was my husband who showed me truths from the Word of God that changed my life.

I found out that it was not Jezebel's makeup or jewelry that made her evil, but it was her wicked heart. I found out that *rules* are man-made and that God operates by the Spirit of the law, not the letter of the law. If we love Him, we will keep His commandments and do His will. I also found out that you can be just as anointed wearing a pantsuit as you can be wearing an ankle-length dress. It's so good to be *free!*

We are now living in a new millennium! God is releas-ing greater revelation and knowledge into the earth. Apostle Williams has been given a mandate from God to enlighten the Body of Christ concerning traditions, especially in the area of women's roles in the church. We know that every woman does not have a five-fold ministry calling. However, whatever God has chosen you to do – whether it is minister-ing in the choir or greeting other people as they enter the church doors – you should be *free* to fulfill your call to the Body of Christ.

As you read this powerful book, I pray that the Holy Spirit will minister to your heart and that you will be con-fronted, challenged, and changed as a result of the anointed revelations herein. Trust me, you will have a brand-new perspective on women in ministry and your life will never be the same!

Sherrilyn R. Williams
Wife of Apostle Alton R. Williams

Preface

My church has been so richly blessed by the ministries of women – those who are members as well as female guest evangelists and prophetesses whom God has sent to minister in our church.

Considering the fact that the majority of members in a church are women, it is likely to believe that women are needed to minister to other women. As male pastors, we sometimes lack the sensitivity toward the needs of women that a female minister can provide. This is not to say that a woman cannot give a word from God to men. By all means she can, has, and should. (The men in my congregation have been extremely receptive to women who have stood before them to preach and teach.)

I have found in my twenty-one years of ministry that women ministers are sometimes more faithful and dependable than some egotistical men ministers. Women lack the ego concerns of their male counterparts. They also bring more of a sensitivity to the things of the Spirit and His gifts than do most men.

I do not want to leave the impression that everything has been perfect with women ministers. Women are imperfect just as men are. Women have their competitive jealousies and sometimes drift away from being under their spiritual covering. However, once pastors learn how to teach and train women who have a ministry calling, many problems will be eliminated. Some of these areas of instruction are God's divine order in the church, proper attitudes toward leadership, balanced submission to male leadership, faithfulness, and servanthood.

Women are looking for a place to go to fulfill their calls and use the gifts God has given them. The church should be an incubator or a launching place and should provide a supportive environment.

One of the main reasons pastors have problems even with their male ministers is a lack of training and teaching. I pray that this book will not only assist women in being free to minister as God calls, but will allow pastors the freedom to know it is all right with God that women be released. Hopefully this book will assist you in your teaching and training in this area.

It will renew the mind and help to clear up many misconceptions brought on by traditions and erroneous teachings.

Introduction

The inspiration for this book officially began for me in December 1993. I had just been appointed Bishop and a founding father of the Full Gospel Baptist Church Fellowship, founded by Bishop Paul S. Morton. The fellowship made the decision to embrace women in ministry and needed an official biblical statement. During our inaugural organizational meeting week that year, the Spirit of God moved upon my heart to write the statement. Of course, a ministry statement has to be limited.

This book contains the detailed revelation God gave me in my hotel room that night, along with further revelation He has given me since that time.

The role of women in the church and in ministry has been the subject of great controversy through the centuries in Church history. Unfortunately, this issue has been dealt with in a severely negative way, depending upon the teachings of denominations or the level of understanding that each pastor or Christian leader has ascertained.

Beliefs concerning women in ministry vary from church to church. I have seen some places that teach women should have total equality with men when it comes to ministry and leadership in the church. Some church denominations do not even allow the women of the church to speak at all during official worship services. Some do not allow any ministry at all by women. A few have learned how to take a somewhat neutral position on this highly controversial issue. The problem with Christians is we have learned to accept the biases of our church's denominational traditions instead of *rightly dividing* (properly and prayerfully dissecting) the Scriptures for ourselves.

With the advent of women's liberation and feminist movements, society is experiencing a reversal of roles as it pertains to women in the home, church, and workplace. Women are looking for fulfillment and purpose. The church should be the one place where they can find their place and destiny.

We live in a world today where women no longer have to be dependent upon the husband's salary. They have high positions in the corporate world and enjoy great paying jobs and careers. As a result, women do not want to be relegated or restricted to the traditional roles of housewife, homemaker, and mother. That spirit of independence and liberation has brought restlessness and resentfulness to the female. Then, before they realize it, they are attempting to become something that God never intended. In today's hectic world, many women become frustrated, trying to be more like their male counterparts.

The prophet Isaiah foretold of a day when there would be a rise of ungodly women's movements that would seek to rule:

> *As for my people, children are their oppressors, and* **women rule over them.** *O my people, they which lead thee cause thee to err, and destroy the way of thy paths.*
>
> Isaiah 3:12

Men must bear great responsibility in this because they have failed to take their God-given leadership in society, the home, and the church. Because of infidelity, abandonment, abuse, rejection, divorce, lack of financial support, spiritual headship and responsibility, many women have sought independence and freedom from their male counterparts.

However, true fulfillment can only be found in obedience to Jesus Christ. A woman will not find her rightful place until she submits herself to the plan, will, and purpose of God for her life, which will involve submission to male headship.

This book has been written to give women hope in knowing that they have been created to walk in a God-ordained purpose. Women are not afterthoughts in the mind of God, yet God has ordained divine order for His Kingdom. Many erroneous traditional teachings will be cleared up in this book and will set those women free who feel they have a call to minister on their lives.

But, this book is not just for women. I encourage men to read it too. Especially men who have been surprised by a wife who suddenly announces, *"Honey, I think I've been called to preach."*

I believe this teaching will enlighten seasoned pastors as well. I, for one, am constantly seeking clarity and a deeper understanding of God's Word. I pray daily that He will open my *spiritual* eyes to things that sometimes just don't *feel* right in my natural state of consciousness. I believe you, too, will be blessed.

1
Women Called by God To Go Forth

The Lord gives the word [of power]; the **women who bear** *and* **publish [the news]** *are* **a great host.**

Psalm 68:11 AMP

I believe this passage of Scripture is prophetically describing the advance of women in ministry during the end times. No other time in history has there been such a great host of women bearing the good news of the Gospel.

The *King James Version* uses the term "company." *"The Lord gave the word: great was the company of those that published it"* (Psalm 68:11). When you interpret this word in the Hebrew, it is interpreted in the female gender. The Hebrew thought is, "Great was the company of women publishers or women evangelists."

Another translator says of this verse, "God gave them His Word (the word of the Lord came unto them), and great was the company of the preachers – prophets and *prophetesses*, for the word 'company' is feminine."

When God has messages to send, He will not lack messengers. Or perhaps it may allude to the women joining in triumph when the victory is obtained, as characterized in Exodus 15:20 and 1 Samuel 18:7. *"The Lord gives the word [of power]; the women who bear and publish [the news] are a great host"* (Psalm 68:11 AMP). The good news or good tidings would be the proclaiming of the Gospel of Christ (Isaiah 52:7, 40:9). This does not sound like silent women to me.

Certain expositors say that the literal rendering of Isaiah 40:9 is, *"O woman, that bearest good tidings...."*

1

This may refer to the women who preached the Gospel, or it may refer to the church as the woman, the bride of Christ, bearing the good tidings to all nations. These things find fulfillment in the New Testament where women labored in the Gospel along with Christ and the apostles.

Tradition Has Brought the Confusion

The church has seen many issues that caused division, separation, strife, and hostility, such as mode of baptism, baptismal formula, wearing of slacks, makeup, and jewelry, musical instruments in the church, divorce, Sabbath day worship, tongues, healing, deliverance, and the list goes on. Another major issue of great concern is the place of women in the ministry.

So what is a woman's place in the ministry? It is no secret that years of improper traditional teaching is the main reason women have been denied their place in the Body of Christ, and denied the right to operate in ministry and spiritual gifts that Paul stated was for the Body (1 Corinthians 12:25-30). There are anointed and gifted women all over this country looking for a place where they can belong and be permitted to give full expression of their gift and call into the ministry.

Satan has robbed the church of many, many years of fruitful ministry from *women of God. Thousands of women* with a call upon their lives have cried, grieved, and struggled within, with a burden and a longing to serve God. Yet, because they feared rejection by churches, pastors, fellow members, family, and friends, many women, like the servant with one talent, have had to hide their talents in the earth (Matthew 25:25).

If one would give careful study to the Scriptures by considering God's whole counsel on an issue, then proper understanding can be received. The greatest amount of confusion has come from 1 Corinthians 14:34-35 and 1 Timothy 2:11. Many church denominations have interpreted those scriptures that say a woman should "keep silent" to mean that she should not preach, teach, or never have any authoritative position over a man in the church. Some groups do not even allow their women to say anything, period!

However, a careful study of the Greek word for "woman" in these passages will prove that the word "wife" was intended. Paul talked about the women learning from their *husbands*. This would be a difficult assignment for single women or for women who had unbelieving husbands, which means all women could not be considered here. I am convinced that what Paul was saying in 1 Timothy is, *"I suffer not a wife to teach or usurp authority over her husband."*

2
Let the Women Learn in Silence

Paul's Epistle to Timothy

*Let the woman **learn in silence** with all subjection.*
*But I suffer not a woman to teach, nor to **usurp authority***
over the man, but to be in silence.

1 Timothy 2:11-12

What's the problem with this scripture? It's simple: We have taken it out of context from the verses around it. Once you break this scripture down by single words and small phrases, the true original intent of the writer will begin to be understood. The historical and scriptural context should also be carefully studied.

Defining "Silence" – vv. 11-12

"Let the woman learn in silence . . . but to be in silence." The Greek word for "silence" is *hesuchia*, which means quietness or to be in stillness; undisturbing, still, peaceable, to keep one's seat. Another definition is to desist from bustle or talk.

If you were to look up other scriptures with this same word "silence," it does not mean absolute silence (See 1 Corinthians 14:28,34; Revelation 8:1; Acts 21:40). In these scriptures, the Greek word means "to hiss or hush."

Timothy knew and understood that Paul was not trying to bring women to absolute silence. (Wouldn't that be a huge task?) He was Paul's son in the faith and he frequently traveled with Paul. He was aware of Paul's position concerning women being allowed to pray and prophesy in the church (1 Corinthians 11:4). Timothy knew about the women in ministry in the Roman church (Romans 16:3-4). He knew about the respect and honor Paul held for Priscilla along with her husband Aquila who taught and pastored a church in their home. He knew about Philip's four daughters who were prophetesses (Acts 21:9). No way could he be telling women now to be totally silent!

Paul is merely saying that the women are to learn in quietness – to be peaceful, restful, and tranquil. He did not mean for them to be mute or to have an oppressive spirit of muteness or dumbness and be completely without communication. It meant to be undisturbed by strife or stillness of spirit. A woman should not strive.

Defining "Subjection" – v. 11

The word "subjection" in the Greek is *hupotasso*, which means to arrange oneself under another. *Hupo* means to be under and *tasso* means to arrange. This primarily declares the same thing Paul was saying in other passages concerning the marital relationship about the women being in submission and subjection (Ephesians 5:22; 1 Peter 3:1). To be in "subjection" means to yield to the preference of others, in this case, her husband. The wife must not demand, assert, or force her authority over her husband.

Defining "Man" - v. 12

The Greek word for "man" in this passage is the word *aner*, which means "the husband." When you consider the context is speaking of the first husband and wife, Adam and Eve, in verses 13-15, the issue is marriage, not ministry in the church.

Defining "Usurping Authority" – v. 12

The Greek word for "usurp" is *authenteo*, which means to seize by force or without right; to force a claim on;

authority that has not been given; to rule over; to dictate to; domineer over. It means the woman is not to be domineering. She is not to have a dominating control over her husband. Paul is saying to married women that they should not practice teaching or dominating their husbands.

Once again we can see the issue is the husband and wife relationship. During this time women were not vocationally trained or educated. They had a need and a right to learn spiritual things. They were to listen to their husbands with a peaceful, contented spirit that was free of confusion and strife, and they were to listen to their husbands' explanations and instructions of spiritual things.

The issue was *never* that women could not preach, teach, lead, or minister, but they were *not* to usurp or take possession by force or seize control or power.

Usurping authority means one who acts upon their own authority when no one has delegated to them that authority. Instead they get up and teach or do things before the congregation without respecting or recognizing the leadership God has already established in the church as well as in their husbands.

Remember, these women were coming out of pagan, female-dominated religions where the women conducted the whole religious rituals and ceremonies. They did all the teachings in these temples. Diana was the mythical goddess of the great temple in the city of Ephesus. Paul is only saying that the women of God should not be like the women of Diana's temple.

Both Jezebel (1 Kings 21) and Athaliah (2 Kings 11) are examples of women who usurped authority that was not given to them (Also see Revelation 2:20).

Keep in mind Paul had to be talking about believing husbands because many unbelieving husbands have been brought to the Lord, saved, and taught by a believing wife. So Paul is not talking about absolute silence of the women. The issue is women *seizing* the authority over the man, whether it is her own husband or male leadership. A woman can act under authority, but she should not force or manipulate herself into a position of authority.

3
Women Keep Silence in the Church

Let your women keep silence in the churches: for it is not permitted unto them to speak; but they are commanded to be under obedience, as also saith the law. And if they will learn any thing, let them ask their husbands at home: for it is a shame for women to speak in the church.

1 Corinthians 14:34-35

This is the next passage of Scripture used against women in ministry. The Corinthian epistle is used primarily to bring order in the church during its public gatherings. The conclusion of 1 Corinthians 14 deals with talkative wives who were disrupting the services by asking their husbands questions while the services were in progress.

Keep in mind that Paul has already given women permission to prophesy and pray in the church (1 Corinthians 11:5). That point alone refutes the issue that women have to be silent and can never say anything. Otherwise it would be a contradiction. We have to consider the whole counsel of Paul's teachings dealing with the women. You have to interpret these scriptures on the "silence of women" in light of its historical setting and customs. This letter was sent to the same church. Let's take a look at this scripture and *rightly divide* it.

"Let your women" – v. 34

Once again this verse cannot be dealing with *all* women. It has to concern the wives because verse 35 tells them to ask their husbands at home. This is not a statement intended for *all* women. All women were not married (1 Corinthians 7:34).

9

All women did not have saved husbands (1 Corinthians 7:13). Therefore, these women did not have men in the church that could instruct them.

Can you see the real issue here? Are there unmarried women in the church today? Are there women in the church today with unsaved husbands? I rest my case.

"Keep silence in the churches" – v. 34

"Silence" in this passage means to be silent, silence, to hush, or to hiss. The best way to help you understand the use of this word is to show you how the same word is used in other passages.

But if there be no interpreter, let him keep silence in the church; and let him speak to himself, and to God.

1 Corinthians 14:28

Notice, when the Spirit of God is in manifestation through speaking in tongues and there is no interpreter, then they are to be *silent*. The same word is used relative to the women. This does not mean that the person speaking in tongues should never speak in tongues again or should never speak period. Paul is giving order for what should be done at that moment when those gifts are in operation.

Let the prophets speak two or three, and let the other judge. If any thing be revealed to another that sitteth by, let the first hold his peace.

1 Corinthians 14:29-30

Paul uses that same "silent" word in reference to prophets who prophesy during the services. If those with a prophetic gift have something revealed to them, then the first one is to be silent so the other one can speak. However, this does not mean that they can never speak again. Paul is giving order for when the gift of prophecy is in operation. If the women want to know what the message was in tongues and prophecy, they should be silent at that moment. Instead of shouting out and asking their husbands for understanding on what was said, they were to be silent.

Yet, as in the other cases where this same "silent" word was used, it did not mean a permanent silence that was forever. Paul demanded a certain order so that the Spirit could give full expression to the people so they could be blessed without any distractions. *This is not a command to silence the women in church and keep them from preaching any more than it is to silence those who speak prophecy or messages in tongues.*

The reason this will be difficult to understand for traditional ministries that are not Spirit filled is because they do not have these things operating in their churches (Acts 2:4). Tradition has caused the confusion on this subject. Without Spirit-filled eyes, there is no revelation.

> *Which things also we speak, not in the words which man's wisdom teacheth, but which the Holy Ghost teacheth; comparing spiritual things with spiritual.* **But the natural man receiveth not the things of the Spirit of God: for they are foolishness unto him:** *neither can he know them, because they are spiritually discerned.*
>
> 1 Corinthians 2:13-14

"For it is not permitted unto them to speak. . . . For it is a shame for women to speak in the church" – vv. 34-35

Once again Paul allowed the women to pray and prophesy in the church in 1 Corinthians 11:5, which involves speaking in the church (1 Corinthians 14:3). You cannot pray and prophesy, especially prophesy, without audible speaking. So Paul cannot come back now and say that they can't speak in the church. That would be a contradiction. Therefore, this passage has to be referring to a specific restricted time and circumstance – that of the husband-wife relationship during services.

There are several Greek derivatives for the word "speak":

Legein – Speaking in an ordinary conversation.

Eipein – An ordered discourse; delivering or speaking forth an ordered discourse.

Lalein – To gabble, talk in an undertone, low tone; to babble or chatter; prattle.

The Greek word for "speak" used in verses 34 and 35 is *laleo*, which means to talk or utter words. In other words, making inarticulate sounds instead of articulate speech that is understandable. Paul was simply telling the women (wives) not to be disorderly in the services and they should not be permitted to gab or talk in an undertone while the Spirit was moving because their chatter would disturb both the speaker and the hearers. (Sounds like a good rule for today's church!) (See Liddel and Scott's Lexicon.)

Try to place yourself in the minds of these women at this time of biblical history. These women have come to Christ out of pagan, heathen religions. They were searching for truth and hungered for it. Their quest for understanding the ways of the Spirit was disturbing the meetings. These women had little or no education and their questions in the service were causing great distraction. Generally the men sat in front of the speaker while the women sat in another part of the sanctuary. In other words, Paul was only telling them, "Be quiet" (for now) and ask your husbands when you get home so the Spirit will not be disturbed." (See Halley's Bible Handbook.)

You know, it's amazing how preachers have used this passage to prove that women could not preach. Yet the word "silence" was used to justify the "no preaching" rule. Think about it. If we were to take this literally as it appears, based upon the traditional understanding we have, women in the church would not be able to sing, teach, pray, speak, etc. Pastors can't afford to do that because they know it would mean the end of their churches since most churches have far more women than men. But not only that, the majority of their finances come from women. What a contradiction this is to their stand against women being silent or their interpretation of Paul's writings.

Once again, Paul is not advocating the absolute permanent silence of women in churches. All he is doing is telling the wives their function during the services. Paul was simply saying that wives were not to disturb the gatherings by the inconvenient asking of questions, talk, and chatter.

"But they are commanded to be under obedience, as also saith the law" – v. 34

Notice, it did not say that the law commanded silence. Instead, it commanded them to be under obedience. You will not find another verse in the prophets or the law of Moses that commands the women to be silent.

Once again, it is only dealing with the *married women* of the church, which is consistent with Paul's other epistles commanding women to obey and submit to their husbands.

> *Wives,* **submit** *yourselves unto your own husbands, as unto the Lord.*
>
> Ephesians 5:22

> *Wives,* **submit** *yourselves unto your own husbands, as it is fit in the Lord.*
>
> Colossians 3:18

> *Likewise,* **ye wives, be in subjection** *to your own husbands; that, if any obey not the word, they also may without the word be won by the conversation of the wives.*
>
> 1 Peter 3:1

That's why Paul had to call for the wives to be obedient. In light of the Corinthian problem, it is scripturally correct to tell the wives, who were disturbing the services, to be under obedience to their husbands and to ask questions about the services at home. In today's language, I believe Paul would have written, *"Wives, don't yell down at your husbands and cause confusion in the services."*

13

Keep in mind the ones who were learning were to keep quiet, not the ones who were teaching. So this is all about wives submitting to their husbands in church, not women preaching or ministering.

4
You Said What?

An Extended Look at the
1 Corinthians 14 "Silent" Scripture

Let me offer you another possible view of 1 Corinthians 14:34-38. I believe Paul could possibly be rebuking the Corinthian men for their prejudice toward women. Keep in mind that Corinthians is a response letter by the Apostle Paul where he is answering some of the many questions that they had sent him to answer. I believe the Corinthian men were trying to get Paul to side with them on the issue concerning their women [wives]. Let me paraphrase what I think they were saying:

> *Paul, we believe that our women should keep silence in the churches and that they should not be permitted to speak, because you know what the law says, how they should be under obedience to their husbands. And Paul, you need to let them know that if they are going to learn anything, they need to wait until they get home and ask their husbands because it is a shame for them to say anything during the services or while the Spirit is moving. They should not prophesy or speak in tongues.*

This makes more sense because why would Paul say in this passage that women should be silent and not speak, yet in another scripture in Corinthians, permit them to speak (1 Corinthians 11:5). This is why I believe Paul was repeating what they had already written to him.

Verse 36 will explain why. Notice how this verse does not fit the flow of the context. Read it and see how it connects with the rest of the passage: *"What? came the word of God out from you? or came it unto you only?"*

To help you understand what or how Paul is saying this, let me give you an example. Suppose I came up to you and made this ridiculous statement: *"All women are stupid and should be locked up in an insane asylum."*

You would be so shocked by the statement that you would possibly repeat what I said, just to make sure you heard me right. After you repeated the statement word for word, you would probably say, *"What?! All women are stupid. . . . What?!"*

I believe that was Paul's surprised reaction in verse 36 to the men saying that women had to be silent and could not speak. Paul said, "What?" Then notice what he asked them. *"Came the word of God out from you? or came it unto you only?"* In other words, "You **(men)** are the only ones that the Word can come from? You **(men)** are the only ones the Word can come out of? How absurd!"

Then, in verse 37 Paul gives them a sharp rebuke: *"If any **man** think himself to be a prophet, or spiritual, let **him** acknowledge that the things that I* [Paul] *write unto you are the commandments of the Lord."*

In essence, Paul was rebuking them for using the law (v. 34) as their premise and trying to restrain women to what the law said. Paul is saying that he is the one that God is speaking through today, under the dispensation of grace and that they should acknowledge that. Throughout Paul's epistles he was always trying to keep the church from reverting back to the law.

> *Knowing that a man is not justified by the works of the law, but by the faith of Jesus Christ, even we have believed in Jesus Christ, that we might be justified by the faith of Christ, and not by the works of the law: for by the works of the law shall no flesh be justified.*
>
> Galatians 2:16

So Paul could not have been advocating the law in verse 34 when he clearly negates the law in Galatians.

Once again, in 1 Corinthians 14:34-35, I believe Paul is repeating or restating what they wrote to him. Then, he rebukes them for their church policy that says a woman could not speak the Word of God or that the Word of God could not come from or through her. Paul lets them know, in no uncertain terms, that they were wrong for thinking that God would only speak through them.

In conclusion, it is not being honest to use 1 Timothy 2 or 1 Corinthians 14 to silence women's ministry in the church through faulty interpretations in light of other biblical revelations of women's roles under God and under headship.

5

Women Allowed To Speak in Other Passages

Every scripture must be interpreted in the light of what other scripture says on the same subject. It must harmonize with all other scripture. If the statement, *"Women must be silent in the church,"* means to say absolutely nothing, why would God allow a woman named Anna, a prophetess (a female prophet), to speak or preach about Jesus right in the temple (or house) of God?

*And there was one **Anna, a prophetess,** the daughter of Phanuel, of the tribe of Aser: she was of a great age, and had lived with an husband seven years from her virginity; and she was a widow of about fourscore and four years, which departed not **from the temple,** but served God with fastings and prayers night and day. And she coming in that instant **gave thanks likewise unto the Lord, and spake of him to all them that looked for redemption in Jerusalem.***

Luke 2:36-38

Women Shall Prophesy

*And it shall come to pass **in the last days,** saith God, I will pour out of my Spirit upon all flesh: and your sons and **your daughters shall prophesy,** and young men shall see visions, and your old men shall dream dreams.*

Acts 2:17

God said that in the last days He would pour out His Spirit upon all flesh; He said your sons and **daughters shall prophesy.** To prophesy means to **speak unto men** edifica-

19

tion, exhortation, and comfort (1 Corinthians 14:3). When one prophesies, **they edify the church** (vv. 4-5). This means if God has poured out His Spirit upon His daughters to prophesy, then they will have to speak to the church. In order to prophesy, you cannot be quiet.

Women were allowed to prophesy and pray during public worship in the church of Corinth.

> But *every woman that prayeth or prophesieth* with her head uncovered dishonoureth her head: for that is even all one as if she were shaven.
>
> 1 Corinthians 11:5

Why would God allow women to speak in one chapter of Corinthians, but tell them to be silent in another?

6

How To Evaluate a God-Ordained Ministry

Paul made a statement in 1 Corinthians 9:1-3 AMP to those Corinthian believers who questioned his ministry and calling. He gave them criteria whereby they could evaluate his ministry:

> **Are you [yourselves]** *(Corinthian believers)* **not [the product and proof of] my workmanship in the Lord?** Even if I am not considered an apostle (a special messenger) by others, at least I am one to you; **for you are the seal (the certificate, the living evidence) of my apostleship in the Lord** [confirming and authenticating it]. This is my [real ground of] defense (my vindication of myself) to those who would put me on trial and cross-examine me.

I believe that if a woman shows proof of a pastorate; if there are people who have been saved, healed, delivered, and set free, or whose lives have been changed as a result of her ministry; if there is fruit and/or growth; if there are women and especially **men** who are willing to submit themselves to her leadership (Hebrews 13:17), then who are we to deny her of her calling? She has, like Paul, a real ground of defense; she has vindication. If there is a product, then there is proof of her workmanship in the Lord. That saved group of believers becomes the evidence, the confirmation, and the vindication of a man or woman's calling.

After years of seeing God move only among the Jewish people, when the time came for God to reach the Gentiles, the Jews had a difficult time receiving them. However, after

Paul saw some evidence of salvation, he said, *"Forasmuch then as God gave them the like gift as he did unto us, who believed on the Lord Jesus Christ; what was I, that I could withstand God?"* (Acts 11:17).

Therefore, who are we, as mere men, that we can withstand God when we see the evidence of a pastorate gift among women – when they possess spiritual gifts as do men. When we see the anointing of God on them as we do the men of God, who are we to question God?

My Mother-in-Law's Ministry

During the early adult years of my life, I, like most Baptists, did not believe in women preachers and pastors – not until I met my wife in 1979. Her mother was a Pentecostal Holiness fireball preacher and pastor! She truly loved the Lord and the people of God. When I saw and heard about the awesome miracles that God wrought through her, my mind changed forever. Many of her members gave testimonies of what God did through her that changed their lives forever. She did things that most male pastors would never do. She was the kind of woman who had compassion for the downtrodden and for the outcast. Her members were the people that most churches, pastored by men, would totally ignore. I saw ex-prostitutes, homosexuals, lesbians, drug addicts, alcoholics, and ex-convicts, all in her church.

I heard about how she would get up in the late night hours and carry groceries to people's houses, give them money, and pay their bills. When some were homeless, she would bring them to her home until they found somewhere else to live. She would pray for people in her home or on the telephone sometimes into the early morning hours. How she prayed and prayed and prayed, which was the source of her power.

Many people were healed by God through this woman of God. Cancers were driven out, legs were lengthened, demons were cast out. I was told of how a well-known local Memphis female celebrity came to her home one night to be prayed for. She had a goiter under her neck the size of a golf ball. My mother-in-law laid hands on that thing, prayed, and cursed it in Jesus' name and right there in her living room that night, it disappeared.

I was also told how one of her members, a prostitute, was trying to make the break from her pimp. She had just recently joined the church. Some way or another my mother-in-law found out that the pimp was holding her against her will and beating on her. She went to the house, stormed through the door, pointed her finger in his face, and demanded that he let her go, leave her alone, and never bother her again.

With gun in hand, something came over him that caused him to get in fear and totally retreat. She left with the girl that night, took her to live in her home for a while, and they never heard from that pimp again. The anointing of God on her life confronted the demon spirits ruling in him and they retreated from her presence.

A woman who was a member of her church got pregnant. The doctors told her according to the ultrasound the baby would be born grotesquely deformed. They tried to convince her to have an abortion. My mother-in-law ministered to her in the hospital and told her not to get the abortion. She laid hands on her, prayed, and believed God. Months later, when the child was born, it was as healthy as any other baby and today is an adult, living a full, normal life.

The ministry of Clithiel L. Ratliff proved to me that God does call women. I wonder what would have happened to all of these people's lives if she had not answered her call. If God is against a person bringing salvation, healing, deliverance, and restoration to someone's life just because she is a female, then I'd rather be an atheist. God is not that narrow, selfish, prejudiced, controlling, religious, and dominating. Religious men are. God would not anoint anyone of whom He disapproved. I cannot see God, supporting with His power, someone doing something contrary to His Word, which is His will. I had to conclude that all of these wonderful testimonies of people giving praise to Jesus had to have been done by the Holy Ghost.

There were times that I felt my old interpretation of scripture concerning women ministers was right. My spirit within was witnessing something different from what the Holy Spirit was saying. I had to stop fighting for my theological, hermeneutical, logical understanding and let myself listen to the spiritual nudging within.

God was using my mother-in-law to prepare me so that my heart would be open to permit women ministers in our church today. Her ministry caused me to look at the scripture again with my eyes and heart open. Rather than just accept what I was told or what I wanted the Scriptures to say, I began to do some deeper study. The Holy Ghost and the Word are going to say the same thing. If the Holy Ghost was confirming her, then I had to be reading the Word wrong.

7

Is It a Sin for a Woman To Lead a Man?

First Timothy 3:1-6 clearly states that a man should be placed in the position of pastor (bishop). We do believe that God's best situation for the office of pastor would be a man, primarily because God has placed into the man the ability to lead.

It would possibly be a little more difficult for a woman to stand in the office of pastor. A woman would have to overcome several obstacles: Societal objections to a woman pastoring; succeeding in her domestic responsibilities as a wife, mother, and homemaker, if she is married (1 Timothy 5:14; Titus 2:3-6); the possible objections of a disagreeable spouse; and finally, women are highly emotional creatures. Her emotions could possibly stand in the way of making pressurized rational decisions in moments of crisis. Yet, I believe God can, has, and will use women in pastoral or leadership positions.

How can we ignore and overlook the fruitful pastoral ministries of women all over this country who confess to having received a call from God to shepherd people and are able to validate that call with results? Jesus said, *"Wherefore by their fruits ye shall know them"* (Matthew 7:20).

Hundreds of people across this land are coming to the Lord through the ministries of women. *If women are wrong for preaching or pastoring, I am sure God will forgive them for getting hundreds of people saved, healed, delivered, and set free by the power of God.* Jesus was saying, in essence, that women who preach for Jesus are not against Him: *"He that is not with me is against me . . ."* (Luke 11:23).

We must keep in mind that God never said that a woman *could not* be a pastor. Whenever God did not want to permit something, He was always straight to the point in His Word. God would specifically say, "Thou shalt not." God never said, "Thou shalt not allow a woman to pastor." God plainly told us who He did not want to be a bishop (pastor) in 1 Timothy 3:6. He only mentioned *a novice*. If God did not want to use a woman at all, I believe this is where He would have placed it and told us.

God has not authorized any of us to judge the ministry of others. I am sure that there are some men who are pastoring who have not been called to pastor. God says our works will be judged at the Judgment Seat of Christ.

> **Who are thou that judgest another man's servant? to his own master he standeth or falleth.** *Yea, he shall be holden up: for God is able to make him stand . . . But why dost thou judge thy brother? or why dost thou set at nought thy brother? for we shall all stand before the judgment seat of Christ . . .*
>
> **So then every one of us shall give account of himself to God.** *Let us not therefore judge one another any more: but judge this rather, that no man put a stumblingblock or an occasion to fall in his brother's way.*
>
> Romans 14:4,10,12-13

Therefore, if any woman, or man for that matter, is pastoring under a false pretense and they have not been called to pastor, only then will there be an honest judgment of a person's heart or calling. If men or women are teaching the Word of God and have a following of submitted people, how can we judge them?

I'm reminded of the words of Gamaliel in Acts 5:39: *"If it* [in this case a woman's ministry] *be of God, ye cannot overthrow it. . . ."* It will come to nought if it is of man (v. 38). Only God can judge who has been disobedient to His call.

If God was against women being in positions of authority over men in the New Testament, then He should have definitely felt that way in the Old Testament. People have said, "Because God placed man over woman in the very beginning, He would never allow a woman to have authority over a man." Let's examine this.

Deborah, the Judge, Rules Israel

In Exodus 18:21,26 Moses' father-in-law gave him some instructions on how to establish a system where he could delegate authority and relieve some of the tremendous pressure he was under as the leader of the camp. Notice the qualifications he gave for those who would be judges (or those in authority):

> *Moreover thou shalt provide out of all the people able* **men,** *such as fear God,* **men** *of truth . . . to be* **rulers.** *. . . And they* **judged** *the people. . . .*

These positions were very similar to the shepherd [pastoral office] in that they had authority over the people. They counseled them and then settled problems and disputes. The Lord said He especially wanted the **men** to be **judges** or **rulers.** However, Judges 4:4 says, *"And Deborah, a prophetess, the* **wife** *of Lapidoth,* **she judged Israel** *at that time."*

Deborah Gave a Man Orders

Deborah led **all of Israel** and was responsible for bringing the people back to God. Deborah, a married woman, was placed in a position of authority, which included having authority over the men. She gave a command to a man named Barak to gather men for battle against Sisera:

> *And* **she sent and called Barak** *the son of Abinoam out of Kedesh-naphtali, and said unto him, Hath not the Lord God of Israel commanded, saying, Go and draw toward mount Tabor, and take with thee ten thousand men of the*

children of Naphtali and of the children of Zebulun? And I will draw unto thee to the river Kishon Sisera, the captain of Jabin's army, with his chariots and his multitude; and I will deliver him into thine hand.

*And Barak said unto her, If thou wilt go with me, then I will go: but if thou wilt not go with me, then I will not go. And she said, I will surely go with thee: notwithstanding the journey that thou takest shall not be for thine honour; **for the Lord shall sell Sisera into the hand of a woman.** And Deborah arose, and went with Barak to Kedesh.*

Judges 4:6-9

Notice what Deborah said in verse 9. She told Barak (one of the men God included in the Hall of Faith in Hebrews 11:32) that he would not get honor or credit for this victory. Instead, she said, *"For the Lord shall sell Sisera into the hand of a woman...."*

God had to prove to men in that day that His work did not have to be done by a man. Deborah's prophecy came true. Another woman named Jael defeated Sisera and killed him.

A Woman, Jael, Defeats the Enemy

In Judges 4:21-22 we read about Jael:

*Then **Jael, Heber's wife took a nail of the tent, and took an hammer in her hand, and went softly unto him, and smote the nail into his temples,** and fastened it into the ground: for he was fast asleep and weary. So he died. And, behold, as Barak pursued Sisera, Jael came out to meet him, and said unto him, Come, and I will shew thee the man whom thou seekest. And when he came into her tent, behold, **Sisera lay dead, and the nail was in his temples.***

God used two women to receive honor for the defeat of Sisera. Deborah started it, and Jael finished it. God said that He would use the weak things to confound the mighty and the woman has been called the weaker vessel (1 Peter 3:7).

Barak (a man) even stated that he would not go on that mission without Deborah. He recognized and depended upon God's anointing upon this woman.

And Barak said unto her, If thou wilt go with me, then I will go: but if thou wilt not go with me, then I will not go.

Judges 4:8

Barak depended on the leadership of a woman. Why would God put a woman in this position of authority when He specifically stated that He only wanted a man? If God cannot find a man or enough men to do a job, He will use a woman.

Other Women God Used To Speak and Lead

There were a number of women whom God called to be His mouthpiece with the prophetic word in their mouth. If God is saying that women should be totally silent, without preaching, leading, or teaching a man, then we should have no examples of Him ever allowing it to happen. We already have Deborah as a witness that this was not the case.

Huldah

Notice how the men pursued Huldah, the prophetess, for direction and a word from God:

*So Hilkiah the priest, and Ahikam, and Achbor, and Shaphan, and Asahiah, **went unto Huldah the prophetess,** the **wife** of Shallum the son of Tikvah, the son of Harhas, keeper of the wardrobe; (now she dwelt in Jerusalem in the college;) and they communed with her.*

And she said unto them, Thus saith the Lord God of Israel, Tell the man that sent you to me, Thus saith the Lord, Behold, I will bring evil upon this place, and upon the inhabitants thereof, even all the words of the book which the king of Judah hath read:

Because they have forsaken me, and have burned

*incense unto other gods, that they might provoke me to anger
with all the works of their hands; therefore my wrath shall be
kindled against this place, and shall not be quenched.*

*But to the king of Judah which sent you to enquire of
the Lord, thus shall ye say to him, Thus saith the Lord God
of Israel, As touching the words which thou hast heard.*

2 Kings 22:14-18

The king sent these men to Huldah to inquire of the
Lord for himself and for the people concerning God's Word
(v. 13). She prophesied to them the word of the Lord to be
sent back to the king (v. 18), which he carried out (2 Kings
23:1-3; also see 2 Chronicles 34:22).

Miriam

Miriam, the sister of Moses and Aaron, was a prophetess and worship leader. She was classified in leadership
with her brothers.

*And **Miriam the prophetess,** the sister of Aaron, took
a timbrel in her hand; and all the women went out after her
with timbrels and with dances. And Miriam answered them,
Sing ye to the Lord, for he hath triumphed gloriously; the
horse and his rider hath he thrown into the sea.*

Exodus 15:20-21

*For I brought thee up out of the land of Egypt, and
redeemed thee out of the house of servants; **and I sent before
thee Moses, Aaron, and Miriam.***

Micah 6:4

Isaiah's Wife

Isaiah's wife was a prophetess also, sharing in her
husband's ministry.

*And I went unto the prophetess; and she
conceived, and bare a son. Then said the Lord to me, call
his name Mahershalal-hash-baz.*

Isaiah 8:3

Women and the Tabernacle

Women were used in the making of the tabernacle of the Lord. The word "assembled" means to be in the host or to serve it.

*And he made the laver of brass, and the foot of it of brass, of the lookingglasses of the **women assembling,** which assembled **at the door of the tabernacle** of the congregation.*

Exodus 38:8

Men and Women Nazarites

The Law of the Nazarite was for women as well as men. Nazarites were consecrated and separated to the Lord for sacred purposes.

*And the Lord spake unto Moses, saying, Speak unto the children of Israel, and say unto them, When either **man or woman** shall separate themselves to vow a vow of a Nazarite, to separate themselves unto the Lord.*

Numbers 6:1-2

A Wise Woman Saved a City from Destruction

*Then cried **a wise woman** out of the city, Hear, hear; say, I pray you, unto Joab, Come near hither, that I may speak with thee. And when he was come near unto her, **the woman** said, Art thou Joab? And he answered, I am he. Then she said unto him, Hear the words of thine handmaid. And he answered, I do hear.*

Then she spake, saying, They were wont to speak in old time, saying, They shall surely ask counsel at Abel: and so they ended the matter. I am one of them that are peaceable and faithful in Israel: thou seekest to destroy a city and a mother in Israel: why wilt thou swallow up the inheritance of the Lord?

And Joab answered and said, Far be it, far be it from me, that I should swallow up or destroy. The matter is not so: but a man of mount Ephraim, Sheba the son of Bichri by name, hath lifted up his hand against the king, even against David: deliver him only, and I will depart from the city. And the woman said unto Joab, Behold, his head shall be thrown to thee over the wall.

Then the woman went unto all the people in her wisdom. And they cut off the head of Sheba the son of Bichri, and cast it out to Joab. And he blew a trumpet, and they retired from the city, every man to his tent. And Joab returned to Jerusalem unto the king.

2 Samuel 20:16-22

A Girl Witnessed to Naaman

A little girl witnessed to Captain Naaman about the true God of Israel who could heal leprosy (2 Kings 5).

Abigail

The woman Abigail gave David the king a word of wisdom. David received that word and saved himself from bloodshed that he would regret in the time he came to his throne (1 Samuel 25).

Women Inherited Land as Did the Men

Land inheritance was always given to male inheritors. Daughters were entitled to receive inheritances if there were no male inheritors.

*Then came **the daughters** of Zelophehad, the son of Hepher, the son of Gilead, the son of Machir, the son of Manasseh, of the families of Manasseh the son of Joseph: and these are the names of his daughters; Mahlah, Noah, and Hoglah, and Milcah, and Tirzah.*

And they stood before Moses, and before Eleazar the priest, and before the princes and all the congregation, by the door of the tabernacle of the congregation, saying, Our father died in the wilderness, and he was not in the company of them that gathered themselves together against the Lord in the company of Korah; but died in his own sin, and had no sons.

Why should the name of our father be done away from among his family, because he hath no son? Give unto us therefore a possession among the brethren of our father.

And Moses brought their cause before the Lord. **And the Lord spake unto Moses, saying, the daughters of Zelophehad speak right: thou shalt surely give them a possession of an inheritance among their father's brethren; and thou shalt cause the inheritance of their father to pass unto them.**

Numbers 27:1-7

(Also see Joshua 15:16-20 and Job 42:14-15.)

* * *

Women were involved in the restoration of the walls of Jerusalem after the Babylonian captivity (Nehemiah 3:12).

* * *

God speaks of His nation Israel as a woman, thus including both men and women under this figure (Jeremiah 3:1-20).

33

8

Women Leaders in the New Testament

God used numerous women in leadership roles in the New Testament.

Philip's Four Daughters

*"And the same man had **four daughters,** virgins, which **did prophesy"** (Acts 21:9).

Priscilla

One of the first missionaries and a leader of the early Church, along with her husband, Aquila, Priscilla and Aquila risked their lives for the Apostle Paul. Priscilla's spiritual maturity and understanding of the faith helped build up the early Church. She co-pastored the church in their home with her husband.

> *Greet **Priscilla** and Aquila, my helpers in Christ Jesus: Who have for my life laid down their own necks: unto whom not only I give thanks, but also all the churches of the Gentiles. Likewise **greet the church that is in their house.** Salute my wellbeloved Epaenetus, who is the firstfruits of Achaia unto Christ.*
>
> Romans 16:3-5

God even honored Priscilla's name before her husband's in at least two other passages of scripture. Usually the man is mentioned first.

> *Salute **Prisca** and Aquila, and the household of Onesiphorus.*
>
> 2 Timothy 4:19

> *And Paul after this tarried there yet a good while, and then took his leave of the brethren, and sailed thence into Syria, and with him **Priscilla** and Aquila; having shorn his head in Cenchrea: for he had a vow.*
>
> Acts 18:18

God used Priscilla to teach and instruct Apollos, a man considered to be an eloquent, mighty man in the Scriptures. Priscilla was allowed to teach a man, which is contrary to our traditional understanding of 1 Timothy 2:12. God would be contradicting Himself if He said for a woman not to teach at all, then use her to teach in another passage. No, the problem is not God, but our blind traditional understanding of that passage.

> *And a certain Jew named Apollos, born at Alexandria, an eloquent man, and mighty in the scriptures, came to Ephesus. This man was instructed in the way of the Lord; and being fervent in the spirit, he spake and taught diligently the things of the Lord, knowing only the baptism of John.*
>
> *And he began to speak boldly in the synagogue: whom when Aquila and **Priscilla had heard, they took him unto them, and expounded unto him the way of God more perfectly.***
>
> Acts 18:24-26

Paul had them both saluted and thanked by the church. "*The churches of Asia salute you. Aquila and **Priscilla** salute you much in the Lord, with **the church that is in their house**"* (1 Corinthians 16:19).

Phebe

> *I commend unto you **Phebe our sister,** which is a servant of the church which is at Cenchrea: **That ye receive her** in the Lord, as becometh saints, **and that ye assist her in whatsoever business she hath need of you:** for she hath been a succourer of many, and of myself also.*
>
> Romans 16:1-2

36

Paul told the Roman church (men and women) to receive Phebe and assist her in whatsoever **business** she has need of. This means she would have to delegate and give orders to the men as well as to the women. Paul did not limit her service or authority just to women.

Euodias and Syntyche

Paul spoke of Euodias and Syntyche as fellow workers in the Gospel:

> *I beseech **Euodias**, and beseech **Syntyche**, that they be of the same mind in the Lord. And I intreat thee also, true yokefellow, **help those women which laboured with me in the gospel**, with Clement also, and with other my fellowlabourers, whose names are in the book of life.*
>
> Philippians 4:2-3

Eunice and Lois

Timothy had a godly grandmother and mother who taught him the Word of God as a child: *"When I call to remembrance **the unfeigned faith** that is in thee, which dwelt first in thy **grandmother Lois**, and **thy mother Eunice;** and I am persuaded that in thee also"* (2 Timothy 1:5).

Other Women in Leadership in the Church

*"And some of them believed, and consorted with Paul and Silas; and of the devout Greeks a great multitude, and of the **chief women not a few**"* (Acts 17:4).

9
When God Can't Find a Man

God could not even find a man to deliver the first message of Jesus' resurrection. Women were the first messengers to tell the world that He had risen (Matthew 28:1-10). Why? Because there were not enough men available. The men (disciples) had either denied Him, betrayed Him, or deserted Him. Self-preservation, ego, reputation, and image caused them to get in fear.

Even today, there are many men who are not answering their call to the work of God. God will use whomever or whatever He can to accomplish His purpose in the earth. *The bottom line is that God wants people saved* (2 Peter 3:9).

Sometimes male pastors have egos, reputations, and ministerial images they feel pressured to uphold. Men are not always prone to obey God at all costs. Most women do not suffer in this way. They possess a sensitivity to the Spirit and a freedom in God that most men do not have. Therefore, when God says to act or move, they tend to move quickly. Tell a man to praise God and he has to look dignified and keep a certain demeanor. Tell a woman to praise Him and she will come out of her shoes, run, jump, shout, lose her weave, scream, or do whatever to praise God.

There is a female pastor in Memphis who was not satisfied with the service of her male trustee board who had been there long before she was elected. She courageously released them all from their positions. Most men pastors would have been too afraid to take that step. They would have been worried about rocking the boat rather than doing what was best for the church. They would have worried about Brother so-and-so with all of his influence in the church

39

turning the people against him and ultimately losing his church. His ego would have been concerned as to what his preacher friends and peers would think if he had church trouble or was turned out of his church.

Yet, here was a woman who had no image or ego to protect, who was sensitive enough to God to trust Him, who took her authority and did what needed to be done. That is why God can sometimes get more out of an anointed woman than He can from a man.

10
Are the Gifts Only for Men?

Another point concerning biblical confirmation for women pastors comes from Ephesians 4:8,11:

> *Wherefore he saith, When he ascended up on high, he led captivity captive, and gave* **gifts unto men** *. . . And he gave some,* **apostles;** *and some,* **prophets;** *and some,* **evangelists;** *and some,* **pastors and teachers.**

In verse 11, Paul gives a list of the various ministry gifts that Jesus gave to men: **apostles, prophets, evangelists, pastors,** and **teachers.** Jesus once again left these gifts for **men.** The key is, what is the Greek definition of the word "men" in this passage? Whenever the Bible mentions the word "men," the Greek gives two distinct definitions. One word is *aner,* which exclusively means the male gender. The other word is *anthropos,* meaning a human being, which is inclusive of the male and female genders. This term encompasses the species of man (male and female).

The Ephesians 4:8 Greek word for "men" is *anthropos,* a term inclusive of both male and female. That means God gave all those gifts – apostles, prophets, evangelists, pastors, and teachers – both to male and female to operate in to bless the Body of Christ and win the lost.

Women Are a Part of Christ's Body

In Romans 12:1-8, God talks about giving every man (*anthropos* – human being) the measure of faith and grace to function in various foundational gifts. *He gives these gifts to His Body.* To say that women are not gifted by God to minister is to say that they are not a part of the Body of Christ.

41

All believers in Christ, whether male or female, are in the Body of Christ.

> *For as the body is one, and hath many members, and all the members of that one body, being many, are one body: so also is Christ.* **For by one Spirit are we all baptized into one body. . . .**
>
> 1 Corinthians 12:12-13

> *There is neither Jew nor Greek, there is neither bond nor free,* **there is neither male nor female: for ye are all one in Christ Jesus.**
>
> Galatians 3:28

Notice the gifts God has given to His Body to use in His Church. Keep in mind, God makes no distinction between male and female in this passage:

> **Now ye are the body of Christ,** *and members in particular. And God hath set some in the church, first* **apostles,** *secondarily* **prophets,** *thirdly* **teachers,** *after that* **miracles,** *then gifts of* **healings, helps, governments, diversities of tongues.**
>
> 1 Corinthians 12:27-28

If women are not allowed to operate in these gifts, then we are saying they are not in the Body. If they are not in the Body, then they cannot be saved. If women are in the Body, then they have been given the right to operate in prophecy, ministering (serving), teaching, exhorting, giving, ruling (administration), or mercy. One of the seven motivational gifts of the church is *ruling. Women in the Body will be in positions of ruling.* If not, God should have said "no" right here.

> *So we, being many, are one body in Christ, and every one members one of another. Having then gifts differing according to the grace that is given to us, whether* **prophecy,** *let us prophesy according to the proportion of faith; or* **ministry,** *let us wait on our ministering: or he that* **teacheth,** *on teaching; or he that* **exhorteth,** *on exhortation: he that*

giveth, let him do it with simplicity; he that **ruleth,** with diligence; he that sheweth **mercy,** with cheerfulness.

Romans 12:5-8

Aimee Semple McPherson

Aimee Semple McPherson founded and pastored a church in Los Angeles, California, in 1923 that led to the establishment of the Four Square Pentecostal Church denomination. Today, years later, there are over 1,500 churches nationwide, and over 3,500 ordained and licensed ministers with 5,000 congregations overseas.

Jack Hayford, pastor of the Church of the Way in Van Nuys, California, is a member of this movement. All of this was birthed out of the anointing God had placed upon a woman. *"If it be of God, ye cannot overthrow it . . ."* (Acts 5:39).

11

Male Headship Is
the Will of God

Please let me reiterate, *I do advocate women submitting to their spiritual and domestic male headship.* I believe that Scripture clearly points to divine order of the man and woman, whether in the natural domestic house or the spiritual house of the Lord, the church. It is important, therefore, to understand biblical headship.

We believe God's best and His established order is a woman functioning under male headship and in this is the safety of the Lord. Headship does not mean superiority or dictatorship of the man or inferiority of the woman or her suppression under the guise of submission. Man is the head of the woman, or the husband is the head of the wife and home (1 Corinthians 11:3). Man and woman together are under the headship of Christ.

Christ is the **man,** the husband, and head of the Church. The Church is the **woman,** the wife and mother (Bride of Christ) (Ephesians 5:23-32; Colossians 1:18, 2:9). "Headship" means authority, order, loving care, discipline, covering, protection, provision, responsibility, and security.

We can see biblical leadership perfectly manifested in the headship of Christ over the Church. It illustrates the order of the home between husband and wife. Therefore, because the Church is considered to be the family of God (Ephesians 3:15), this order should be illustrated in the Church, the house of the Lord. God's prescribed order then would be a woman gifted of God ministering and exercising spiritual authority as she acts under male authority. However, this does not mean that she could never hold a position of authority.

A. A woman preaching, teaching, and ministering through the gifts of the Spirit and the ministry of helps to women and/or men in the church under the authority of her male pastor, is in order (Luke 2:36-38).

B. A woman co-pastoring with her husband, yet under his authority and covering, is in divine order (Romans 16:3-4).

C. A woman sent to evangelize or to work on the mission field with the blessing and covering of her pastor and church is in divine order.

In summary, a woman under male leadership, either her husband's and/or church leadership, is acting under authority and not usurping authority. This is God's divine order.

12
God's Plan B

I shall never forget watching the last episode of "Roots" when Chicken George came and rescued his family from the prejudiced white landowners. They had set up an ambush against old Mr. Brent that did not work. Brent brought his backup posse, and the first planned ambush failed. When they went to the barn to find the rest of the family, Brent and his men were ambushed a second time. I remember Chicken George saying what his old military army general said, "What do you do when your first plan fails? Get yourself another plan." In other words, have a Plan B ready in the event Plan A does not work.

When man fell in the Garden of Eden, it was God's intent and first plan (Plan A) that man would live under obedience to Him and to His purpose. However, man chose to follow his own plan and decided to eat from the tree. Now sin was passed down to all mankind (Romans 5:12). God had to come up with a Plan B to redeem man. God Himself had to come into the earth wrapped in human flesh to die for mankind. No other man in the earth was without sin to die for the world. Only God could do it. When Plan A did not work, God resorted to His Plan B.

Let me give you an example closer to home. Let's say you rear a daughter in the fear and admonition of the Lord. You teach her morals, right and wrong, the ways of God, etc. You teach her about men and sex. You warn her about fornication and pregnancy before marriage. You make your threats such as, "If you get pregnant, you'll have to take care of that child on your own. I won't be taking care of any babies. You'll have to get your own place because there will not be any out-of-wedlock babies in this house." Your Plan A is children growing into adulthood, getting married, and then having children. That would have been the right way, the best way, God's way.

Then, one day your daughter comes home with those horrible, unexpected words: "I'm pregnant." After you get over your anger, after all of the tension and tears, after nine months, you look down in the face of that innocent grandchild and all of the things you said under Plan A go straight out of the window. You clear out one of the rooms, purchase baby furniture, paint the room, and put up cartoon curtains to make room for your grandchild. What you said you would not do, love forced you to a Plan B. Sometimes original plans have to be altered.

God's plan has always been for the man to be in headship. The man in leadership has always been God's best. God created man to lead. Yet, God will resort to a Plan B when He has to. God was even willing to break the course of nature and speak through an ass when He needed a word to be spoken (Numbers 22:28).

Why are we seeing such a vast number of women called to the preaching or pastoring ministry? I believe that because of sin, many men are not operating in their God-given calls and God is looking for willing vessels to get His Word out. God's main concern is that people hear the Gospel message and get saved. This is not to say that women are an afterthought with God, but His best plan has always been men in headship over women.

13

God Had To Use Women To Lead in the Home

Let's look at the natural home. As stated earlier, God's best and original intent is the man, husband, or father in headship in the home, leading, guiding, and directing his family. This is God's best, His divine order, and as stated earlier, it should be the same design in the Church.

However, what about a woman whose husband divorces or abandons her and leaves her with several children to take care of? What about the young girl who had one or more children out of wedlock? These women are all forced to raise children without a husband or a father. God's best or original intent was for a man to lead that home and help to raise those children. We are living in a world today where that is not the case.

Today, many children are being raised in single-parent homes led by females. Although it is not God's best, many children, as well as adults, have been raised by a woman. The mother in that home had to be man and woman, mother and father. She had to work to feed, teach, train, discipline, and correct the children. She had to teach them about God and take them to church herself.

Many women have successfully raised great, stable, God-fearing children. Although it was not God's best, God used that single mother to prepare His heritage for life. Many preachers who are in pulpits today were reared by women who taught and preached to them about Jesus. Not one time have I heard a preacher say, "We cannot have a woman leading or teaching her male children in the home."

If we trust a woman to teach, train, tell us about God, and lead us in the home, why can't we trust her to tell us about God in the church? We could trust her prayers and Bible story teaching in the home, but not in the church. We won't allow women to carry the Word to sinners from their mouths, yet God could trust Mother Mary to carry **The Word** in her womb.

In summary, God's plan for the natural home was male headship, but when that headship is not there, God has to use women to rear His children. God's plan for the spiritual house is the same as the natural house. But when the male headship is not there and God has a vessel willing to obey Him, get the Word to His people and nurture them, what do you think God will do? God anoints women in the home to get the job done. He can do the same in His Church when He needs to.

My Summary Position on Women Pastors

Because we have biblical evidence of a woman operating in a position of authority over men, we realize that we cannot lock God into a box and say that God would never use a woman in a pastoral capacity. God is God all by Himself and He will use whatever or whomever He pleases to accomplish His purpose.

To sum up my position on women in ministry, *I believe God's gifts are given without regard to ethnicity, social class, or gender* (Ephesians 4:7-12; Galatians 3:26-28). We have proven Scripture teaches that women operated as prophetesses in the Old and New Testaments (Exodus 15:20; Judges 4:4; 2 Kings 22:14; Nehemiah 6:14; Isaiah 8:3; Luke 1:39-56; 2:36; Acts 21:8-9; 1 Corinthians 11:4-5). They were involved in the ministry of helps (1 Corinthians 12:28; Romans 16), and they were leaders in the church (Philippians 4:2-3; Romans 16:1-2).

As it pertains to women pastors, because the Word of God has never given a commandment against female pastors and because there is scriptural evidence of women being in positions of authority, I believe that if a female pastor has the following criteria in evidence in her life, who are we to withstand God?

◆ She has a proven ministry, meaning that people have come to the Lord through her ministry and are willing to submit themselves to her leadership (1 Corinthians 9:1-3; Hebrews 13:17);

◆ She operates properly under her domestic covering, being in agreement with her spouse concerning her ministry, if she is married (1 Corinthians 11:3; Amos 3:3; Ephesians 5:24);

◆ She preaches and teaches the doctrines of Christ (2 John 7-11); and

◆ There is a recognition of giftings and the anointing of the Holy Ghost upon her life.

God has not given us the authorization to judge the pastorate calling of any person, male or female, unless the message preached is contrary to Scripture (Romans 14:10-13; 1 Corinthians 3:13; 1 John 4:1).

If God can use a rod (Exodus 4:2,17), if He was willing to step outside the course of nature and speak through an ass (Numbers 22:28), if He could use a ram's horn (Joshua 6:5), an ox, goad, nail, barley cake, pitchers, jawbone, millstone (Judges 3:31; 4:21; 7:13,20), a raven and a little boy's lunch, why is it so hard to believe that God can use a woman?

14

What If I'm Called But My Husband Is Against It?

Many women today carry a call in their hearts to preach the Gospel but are denied the opportunity because of a disagreeing husband. The question I have heard women ask many times is, "How do I obey God which will possibly cause me to disobey my husband?"

This question was answered for me when a woman minister came to me and asked me about a calling on her life that her husband was vehemently against. She said she knew God was calling her to preach and ultimately become an evangelist. She had even received it in several prophecies as well. Her husband told her if she ever preached he would leave her. So she asked, "What do I do, Pastor? Do I obey my husband and miss my calling, or do I obey God and lose my husband?"

I told her the only answer I had was the Word of God. What does the Word say? I said, "I don't have a scripture that I can go to that can prove that you are called. However, I do have scripture on what God says your relationship should be with your husband:

*Likewise, ye **wives, be in subjection to your own husbands;** that, if any obey not the word, they also may without the word be won by the conversation of the wives.*

1 Peter 3:1

Therefore as the church is subject unto Christ, so let the wives be to their own husbands <u>in every thing</u>.

Ephesians 5:24

I told her that God says to be subject to her husband in all things, even if he doesn't know the Word. I told her to go back, pray, obey God's Word, trust Him, and put the ball back in God's court. She went back and got on her knees and prayed to God. She told me that she told God:

> *Lord, You have got to show me what to do. I didn't ask for this call and I did not come looking for a call to preach. I'm not in a hurry to be a preacher. My husband does not want me to preach, and You told me to submit myself to him in Your Word. I do have Your Word so that's what I am going to do and obey.*
>
> *I give my husband's heart to You. I put my trust in You. If You have truly called me as I believe You have, You change my husband's heart and allow him to release me. That will be my final confirming word of Your call. You told me to obey my husband. Therefore, if You can change him, then I know without a shadow of a doubt that You have called me. It's in Your hands.*

She said that when she got up off of her knees, she had a peace that passes all understanding. She said the load was gone. It was now on God and her husband. She stated, "I'm not in a hurry to go out and preach. I don't want to have to face all of this persecution I'm going to have to face anyway. So God, if You want me to preach, You work it out in my husband's heart, because if I do the contrary, our home will not be unified and I don't want our prayers to be hindered in any way."

> *Can two walk together, **except they be agreed?***
>
> Amos 3:3

> *Likewise, ye husbands, dwell with them according to knowledge, giving honour unto the wife, as unto the weaker vessel, and as being heirs together of the grace of life; **that your prayers be not hindered.***
>
> 1 Peter 3:7

A few months later her husband was involved in a car accident that should have taken his life. One day while in the hospital in critical condition, he had her to come near his bedside. He held her hand and began to repent and cry over some things he had done to her during their marriage. He apologized to her and asked her to forgive him. Then he said to her, "I've been wrong for holding you back from your calling and ministry. Since I've been on this hospital bed, God has been dealing with my heart. I've had to repent to Him. So today I'm releasing you to begin preaching."

You might be asking, "Did God cause the accident in order to humble him and release her?" No, I do not believe that. If that were the case, women would start believing God for car accidents for their husbands to get them to change. However, I do believe that God took this mishap, whether it was by human frailty or by Satan, as the opportunity when this man's heart was more contrite to speak to him. Sometimes we can't hear the Lord speak until we are down. We become more sensitive to His voice and His will simply because we are looking for answers as to how we got down. David said, *"It is good for me that I have been afflicted; that I might learn thy statutes"* (Psalm 119:71).

The moral of this story is that if you are married and you have a call upon your life with which your spouse does not agree, you do not have to fight your way into the ministry and bring strife into your home. If God has called you, trust Him to bring it to pass. It's God's job to see to it that it happens. He has ways of getting your husband's attention, and He knows how to change a person's heart.

> *The **king's heart is in the hand of the Lord**, as the rivers of water: **he turneth it whithersoever he will.***
> Proverbs 21:1

The king in this passage represents anyone in authority over you. God can turn the heart of the king in your house, but you must put total trust in Him. If you do anything to control your own situation through manipulation, domination, control, or rebellion in your home, God will not be able to intervene on your behalf. If you are going to be the god of your own situation, then you tie God's hands. However, when your trust is fully in Him without your trying to influence or manipulate your husband, God is free to do some supernatural things on your behalf. All you have to do is pray, trust, submit, and obey.

Keep in mind, a minister's home life and character are more important to God than his or her ministry. God made the family in the Garden of Eden before He made the Church. The only reason the Church was needed was because the family (Adam and Eve) messed up.

15

What If My Pastor Teaches Against Women Preachers?

Many women have asked me, "What should I do if my pastor does not believe in women preachers?" I have had women call our ministry and ask for information on women in ministry that they could give to their pastor, deacons, and members to convince them that it is all right for women to preach.

It is absolutely wrong to try to change a church or bring or teach something contrary to the teachings of that pastor. God honors and respects the authority He has placed in a church. He and only He can change the heart of a man. He and He alone will judge His servants whether they be right or wrong (Hebrews 13:17).

When a woman tries to influence, manipulate, dominate, or control a pastor, that's when she is in violation of **usurping male authority** (1 Timothy 2:12), or trying to force her authority on the pastor, which is exactly what Jezebel did to her husband Ahab's throne (1 Kings 21).

If you are a female with a call to preach and your pastor is against women preachers, you have one of two choices: 1) Stay and pray for him in obedience without causing discord among the brethren (Proverbs 6:19), or 2) Leave and find a pastor and church that do believe in women preachers where your call can be developed and nurtured. If you cause discord in a church regardless of whether the pastor is right or wrong, your ministry will never be blessed. You must never be guilty of causing discord or scattering God's flock and causing them to be driven away (Jeremiah 23:1-2).

Although I do believe that God would forgive a woman who might go into the ministry or pastorate without His call, that still does not mean there will not be consequences. Many women, because of their desire to lead or to be over some people so they can have their way, have failed miserably because God did not call them. There was no fruit of a ministry: no growth, no changed lives, no anointing from God.

Many end up breaking under the weight and pressure of a work that God never called them to. Some have experienced broken homes and marriages, nervous breakdowns, oppression, sickness, or premature death. Some have had their doors closed or have seen their flock scatter because there was no protection from God.

When it is not of God, it will come to nought [nothing] (Acts 5:38). This is especially the case when women begin a ministry in rebellion and split a church to gather their own following (Acts 5:36-37). They start pointing out all of the things the pastor is or is not doing to a few people they influence. Then, they begin gathering people to a so-called prayer meeting for the pastor. That woman's ministry is doomed before it ever gets started.

That's why it is so important that you are prayed up so that you will not miss the voice of God and make a mistake in the flesh.

16
Wisdom for Women in Ministry

Here are seven wisdom guidelines for women in ministry:

1. Have your home in divine order, for how can you minister in the house of the Lord when your own home is out of order? You don't leave your first ministry in the home to go save the world (Titus 2:4-5).

2. Be scripturally qualified as a godly woman with character qualities (1 Timothy 3:1-7).

3. Be scripturally gifted and anointed of the Lord (Ephesians 4:11-12; Romans 12:4-7; 1 Corinthians 12:8-10).

4. Be under male leadership, either your husband's and/or church leadership, so that you are acting under authority and not usurping authority (1 Peter 3:1-2; 1 Timothy 2:12; Titus 2:4-5).

5. Recognize, respect, and accept God's order. First the man, then the woman, as noted in order in Creation, the Fall, Redemption, the home and the church (1 Corinthians 11:3).

6. Beware of humanistic philosophy that teaches "women's liberation," "feminist movements," and rebellion against male leadership in the home, church, or society.

7. Be an example of a godly woman in word, deed, and character to all other women in the house of the Lord and the home. The woman should beware of having a "masculine" spirit, even as the man must beware of having a "feminine" spirit. Today, many women are "mannish" in their approach to ministry while men are "womanish" because of much reversal of roles and the unisex mentality.

Be Led by the Spirit
Concerning Your Ministry

Every woman should be led by the Holy Spirit as it relates to a call in the ministry. This book is not intended to release every woman to go preach or start a church just because you have now found out that God does not condemn women ministers. You must make sure that you are called or you will fall. I wrote this book primarily to dispel erroneous traditional theology that said women could not minister or lead. I pray that it will also open the hearts of pastors blinded by tradition.

There are many women looking for equality in leadership with men. Any theology that locks you into believing that all women ministers are supposed to hold equal leadership positions with men in the church will lead to deception. In many churches, I have seen a sickness creep into some groups that cling to this doctrine. I have seen many women who, without realizing it, received a demonic influence of superiority and pride. Women who are frustrated with their irresponsible, spiritually feeble husbands tend to congregate to these kinds of churches and a disgust and even a hatred toward men develops. I've been grieved and hurt to see how many divorces and bad marriages result in these kinds of Christian churches. Even the men of these churches become more oppressed and spiritually weak. It opens the door for homosexual spirits among men and for spirits of control and witchcraft among the women.

Beware of the Jezebel Spirit

Many so-called women prophetesses who are not under authority of anyone are operating under a "Jezebel spirit."

*Notwithstanding I have a few things against thee, because thou sufferest that woman **Jezebel, which calleth herself a prophetess,** to teach and to seduce my servants to commit fornication, and to eat things sacrificed unto idols.*

Revelation 2:20

60

Jezebel was the domineering, evil wife of King Ahab. The Jezebel spirit, along with the world's concept of the liberated woman, has found access into the hearts of many Christian women today. It was Jezebel who usurped her husband's authority (1 Kings 21).

There is a very fine line between Charismatic religious witchcraft and satanic oriented witchcraft. Both involve control, manipulation, and domination. Many women, who call themselves prophetesses, if not led by the Holy Spirit, will yield to familiar spirits when it comes to giving prophecies. They will use it to seduce, entice, and control people's lives.

The one temptation that has existed in the heart of almost every woman since the Garden of Eden is to get out from under her authority and covering. That's why the first commandment God gave to woman after the fall was, *"And thy desire shall be to thy husband, and he shall rule over thee"* (Genesis 3:16).

God knew that with the presence of sin in Eve, there would be the desire to rebel against her authority and headship. Eve got out from under her husband's covering because of her desire for power, knowledge, and wisdom.

> *And **when the woman** saw that the tree was good for food, and that it was pleasant to the eyes, and **a tree to be desired to make one wise,** she took of the fruit thereof, and did eat, and gave also unto her husband with her; and he did eat.*
>
> Genesis 3:6

That's why witchcraft is such a female-dominated religion today. The psychic phenomena is controlled by women who, like Eve, seek power, knowledge, wisdom, and control. They need something that will give them an edge over their male counterparts to whom God has given His authority. So they seek power outside of the Kingdom of God.

And it came to pass, as we went to prayer, a certain **damsel** *possessed with* **a spirit of divination** *met us, which brought her masters much gain by soothsaying.*

Acts 16:16

The word "divination" means python. The spirit behind witchcraft and psychics is the serpent or the snake, which is symbolic of Satan. This means the same spirit (Satan) that led Eve away from her covering is the same spirit that seeks to lead women away from their God-given authority and covering today.

Remember, woman of God, there is order, care, discipline, protection, provision, and security when you are submitted to a God-ordained spiritual and/or domestic covering. The Jezebel spirit hates all male authority and despises any and all headship whether it be a father, spouse, boss, or pastor. Only a godly woman can submit to God by submitting to those God has set in authority over her.

May God bless you in your quest, woman of God, as you seek to obey and serve Him.

17

Must Women Have Their Heads Covered During Church Services?

But I would have you know, that the head of every man is Christ; and the head of the woman is the man; and the head of Christ is God. Every man praying or prophesying, having his head covered, dishonoureth his head.

But every woman that prayeth or prophesieth with her head uncovered dishonoureth her head: *for that is even all one as if she were shaven. For if the woman be not covered, let her also be shorn: but if it be a shame for a woman to be shorn or shaven, let her be covered.*

For a man indeed ought not to cover his head, forasmuch as he is the image and glory of God: but the woman is the glory of the man. For the man is not of the woman; but the woman is of the man. Neither was the man created for the woman; but the woman for the man. For this cause ought the woman to have power on her head because of the angels.

Nevertheless neither is the man without the woman, neither the woman without the man, in the Lord. For as the woman is of the man, even so is the man also by the woman; but all things of God.

Judge in yourselves: is it comely that a woman pray unto God uncovered? Doth not even nature itself teach you, that, if a man have long hair, it is a shame unto him? But if a woman have long hair, it is a glory to her: for her hair is given her for a covering. But if any man seem to be contentious, we have no such custom, neither the churches of God.

1 Corinthians 11:3-16

There are several denominations or religious groups that believe that women must wear some type of hat or head covering over their heads. I have personally known women

63

who were a part of this type of church that had a fear of removing their hats in the church because of violating this passage. The real question we must answer is whether or not this tradition is still binding for the church today.

I am so glad Paul did not say that not keeping this tradition was irreverent, disrespectful, or displeasing to God. Why? Because if Paul made this a command to the church, then there would have been no getting out of it.

Once again, as with the issue concerning women in ministry, this is a husband and wife issue relevant to the customs of that day. It is not a woman question, but a husband and wife question.

There are different religious customs observed all over the world. In our country, it is not customary for a man to wear a hat or cap in the services, but if you were to go to a Jewish synagogue style of worship, the men wear hats or small caps. In Islamic-Muslim countries, those who worship must take off their shoes.

The custom in Paul's day required women to wear veils or head coverings as a visible acknowledgment that someone present at that service was her head. This means if a man were to wear a covering on his head, in this custom, he would be saying that there was someone physically present as his head.

> *Every man praying or prophesying, having his head covered, dishonoureth his head.*
> 1 Corinthians 11:4

Notice who the man's head is:

> *But I would have you know, **that the head of every man is Christ;** and the head of the woman is the man; and the head of Christ is God.*
> 1 Corinthians 11:3

Christ is the head of every man. However, He is not physically present in the services.

Paul stated that a woman who prayed or prophesied with her head uncovered dishonored her "head." He didn't say she dishonored God, but her head. According to 1 Corinthians 11:3, who is the woman's (wife's) head?

64

> *But I would have you know, that the head of every man*
> *is Christ; and the head of the woman is the man; and the*
> *head of Christ is God.*   1 Corinthians 11:3

According to that custom, the veil covering or hat was only a symbol of a wife's subjection to her husband. When a bride wears a veil today in the marriage ceremony, it stems from this tradition. It was demonstrating the wife's private and subordinate position to her husband. Women are being beaten in Afghanistan at the time of this writing for not wearing their veils in public.

> *For the man is not of the woman; but the woman of the*
> *man. Neither was the man created for the woman; but the*
> *woman for the man.*   1 Corinthians 11:8-9

Because of the reasons stated in these two scriptures, should not the wife demonstrate a sign of her husband's authority, a covering on her head, which is what the custom required?

Once again, this is not a woman issue, but it is a husband and wife issue. In order to give honor and respect to Christ, who is the head of man, the man should not cover his head. Out of respect and honor for her husband, a wife should cover her head and let others know she is taken and already under someone's authority.

Verse 10 speaks of a woman having power on her head, which means authority. It also mentions giving respect to the angels who were present at the public worship services. Angels are there to carry out the will and presence of God in a service. If there was any disorder in the services, it would grieve the angels and could jeopardize their presence.

If a married woman wore a covering, it was a badge of subjection to her husband. If she were married and did not have on her veil covering, people would have thought that she was an immoral woman. This behavior would have dishonored her and her husband.

Paul gave respect to the customs of people. If you are going to be a missionary sent to a foreign country to be a witness for the Lord Jesus Christ, you have to respect their customs. Thank God the Apostle Paul did not bind the churches of God to this practice.

> *But if any man seem to be contentious,* **we have no such custom, neither the churches of God.**
>
> 1 Corinthians 11:16

Weymouth's Translation says, **"But if any one is inclined to be contentious on the point** (*of women wearing head coverings*)**, we have no such custom, nor have the Churches of God."** In other words, Paul is saying as God's Church, we believe and respect the customs of a nation, but it is not a binding commandment or law placed on God's Church. This will assist you in a further understanding of women being silent in the church. It was a custom of that day in public worship.

In summary, the Word of God never said that it was displeasing to Him that women would appear with their heads uncovered. Paul believed it to be wise to respect the customs of a people, but this is not a universal practice of the Church. If you were in a place where this custom was conducted, it would be wise for you to abide by it. Remember Paul's words in 1 Corinthians 9:19-23:

> *For though I be free from all men, yet have I made myself servant unto all, that I might gain the more. And unto the Jews* **I became as a Jew, that I might gain the Jews; to them that are under the law, as under the law, that I might gain them that are under the law; to them that are without law,** *as without law, (being not without law to God, but under the law to Christ,)* **that I might gain them that are without law. To the weak became I as weak, that I might gain the weak:** *I am made all things to all men, that I might by all means save some. And* **this I do for the gospel's sake,** *that I might be partaker thereof with you.*

18

Is It a Sin for Women
To Wear Makeup?

Let's take a look at scriptures that deal with the subject of makeup. The Bible does not use the term "makeup"; instead, it uses the term "paint," "painting of the eyes or face," or "adorning of the physical being." This will be helpful not only to women in general, but to women in ministry who must represent the Lord with excellence, modesty, and moderation.

*And when Jehu was come to Jezreel, Jezebel heard of it; and she **painted her face,** and tired her head, and looked out at a window.*

2 Kings 9:30

This one passage of scripture has been used by those who are proponents against women wearing makeup. Many of these beliefs stem from distorted views of holiness and sexuality. Many women have combined their negative sexual experiences with their doctrines of holiness. If a woman has had bad experiences with men or if their image of themselves sexually has been damaged, that belief will be interwoven into their doctrinal understanding of God.

This, along with traditional beliefs concerning vows of chastity passed down from the Catholic church, has damaged many women when it comes to the subject of adorning and makeup. If a person does not feel good about themselves sexually and they have not been given balanced teaching on the subject of sex, they are going to be against anything that they think will make themselves beautiful or

67

attractive. They feel that attractiveness draws attention from the opposite sex. They think makeup will make one look sexy and therefore cause men to lust. Keep in mind, there are many women who are beautiful, attractive, and sexy without makeup.

Religion has tried to use the Jezebel scripture as proof that makeup is wrong and sinful. Since Jezebel was a sinful woman and used makeup to seduce, tempt, or allure men, that makes it evil. However, the Scriptures did not say that. Jezebel was a mother. Does that make motherhood evil? It also says Jezebel tired or dressed her hair up. Is a nice hairstyle sinful? Jezebel's sin was not the makeup worn outwardly on the body. It was her evil heart. Her sin did not emanate from the outward man. Instead, it originated from the heart.

> For the Lord seeth not as man seeth; for man looketh on the outward appearance, **but the Lord looketh on the heart.**
>
> 1 Samuel 16:7

> There is nothing from without a man, that entering into him can defile him: but **the things which come out of him, those are they that defile the man** . . . And he saith unto them, Are ye so without understanding also? Do ye not perceive, that whatsoever thing from without entereth into the man, it cannot defile him . . .

> And he said, That which cometh out of the man, that defileth the man. **For from within, out of the heart of men, proceed evil thoughts, adulteries, fornications, murders, thefts, covetousness, wickedness, deceit, lasciviousness, an evil eye, blasphemy, pride, foolishness: all these evil things come from within, and defile the man.**
>
> Mark 7:15,18,20-23

Outwardly, things such as makeup cannot defile a woman. That which is within a person's heart is what defiles them. If sexual sin such as fornication and adultery is in the heart and a woman uses makeup as enticement to carry out her sin, then that is evil. I believe any woman who uses her makeup with the intent of the heart to seduce or tempt someone to sin, then her makeup is only used to help carry out the sin in her heart. Keep in mind, the sin is not the makeup. *It is the intent of the heart.*

Makeup is never listed in any of the lists of sins that Paul gives in the New Testament (1 Corinthians 6:9-10; Galatians 5:19-21; Ephesians 5:3-5). The Word of God never gives a direct commandment against makeup. Whenever God did not want a thing, He would say, *"Thou shalt not."* He would speak a direct command against a thing. In some places, He was so adamant about an issue He would preface it with the phrase, *"Let no man deceive you."* He wanted to make sure that there would be no confusion and all "ifs," "ands," and "buts" were settled.

Scripture is clear that lying, murder, stealing, idolatry, fornication, adultery, homosexuality, witchcraft, drunkenness, hatred, strife, and slothfulness are all contrary to the will of God. We can find commandments in the Word of God against these and many other things. However, you will never find a commandment against makeup anywhere in Scripture.

Jezebel's sins were heart related, which caused her to use these things in her seductions.

> *And it came to pass, when Joram saw Jehu, that he said, Is it peace, Jehu? And he answered, What peace, so long as the whoredoms of thy mother Jezebel and her witchcrafts are so many?*
> 2 Kings 9:22

The sins that brought God's judgment on Jezebel were idolatry, whoredom, and witchcraft, all of which are sins of the heart. As a matter of fact, each of the scriptures on the subject of painted face or eyes dealt with the sins of the heart first. The makeup was used as a result of the adultery in the heart. Most women who wear makeup do not have this inward motivation. Most women only want to enhance their appearance or cover some skin flaws they are not proud of on their face. If a man should still lust, that's not her problem, but his.

> *The Lord said moreover unto me; Son of man, wilt thou judge Aholah and Aholibah? yea, declare unto them their abominations; that they have committed **adultery,** and blood is in their hands, and with their **idols** have they committed **adultery,** and have also caused their sons, whom they bare unto me, to pass for them through the fire, to devour them. Moreover this they have done unto me: they have **defiled my sanctuary** in the same day, and have profaned my sabbaths.*
>
> *For when they had slain their children to their **idols,** then they came the same day into my sanctuary to profane it; and, lo, thus have they done in the midst of mine house. And furthermore, that ye have sent for men to come from far, unto whom a messenger was sent; and, lo, they came: for whom thou didst wash thyself, **paintedst thy eyes** and **deckedst thyself with ornaments,** and satest upon a stately bed, and a table prepared before it, whereupon thou hast set mine incense and mine oil.*
>
> Ezekiel 23:36-41

Notice, not only did they paint their eyes, but they decked themselves with jewelry. If makeup is wrong, then the jewelry has to be wrong.

Aholah and Aholibah were judged by God, not because of their eyes being painted, but because of their adultery and idolatry. The adultery in the heart caused them to seduce men.

In Jeremiah 4, God's message to Israel's women was because of their sin and evildoings (vv. 1-4). God was saying, "Though you try to deck yourself with jewelry or paint your face to look fair, your lovers will still despise you."

> *Though thou **clothest** thyself with crimson, though thou **deckest** thee with ornaments of gold, though thou*

*rentest thy **face with painting,** in vain shalt thou make thyself fair; thy lovers will despise thee, they will seek thy life.*   Jeremiah 4:30

Once again, if painting the eyes is being condemned by God in this passage, then He has to also condemn putting on clothing and jewelry, which is mentioned in this scripture. We know that is not what God is saying. *The issue is the sin of the heart.*

Beauty and Adornment

Does God have a problem with a woman adorning herself and being beautiful? In Ezekiel 16, God rebukes Israel for its abominations against Him (vv. 1-2). Then He causes the prophet to reflect back and remind Israel of His blessings and goodness toward them. God gives analogies of how He dressed Israel as a bride adorns herself for her lover or groom.

*Now when I passed by thee, and looked upon thee, behold, thy time was the time of love; and I spread my skirt over thee, and covered thy nakedness: yea, I sware unto thee, and entered into a covenant with thee, saith the Lord God, and thou becamest mine. Then washed I thee with water; yea, I throughly washed away thy blood from thee, and I anointed thee with oil. **I clothed thee also with broidered work,** and shod thee with **badgers' skin,** and I girded thee about **with fine linen,** and I covered thee with **silk.***

*I **decked thee** also **with ornaments,** and I put **bracelets upon thy hands,** and **a chain on thy neck.** And I put **a jewel on thy forehead,** and **earrings in thine ears,** and **a beautiful crown upon thine head.***

*Thus wast thou **decked with gold and silver;** and thy raiment was of fine linen, and silk, and broidered work; thou didst eat fine flour, and honey, and oil: and **thou wast exceeding beautiful,** and thou didst prosper into a kingdom. And thy renown went forth among the heathen for thy beauty:*

for it was perfect through my comeliness, **which I had put upon thee, saith the Lord God.**

Ezekiel 16:8-14

Although this is an analogy, it does demonstrate God's desire in having people of beauty. He adorns Israel as a woman adorns herself with beautiful clothing, bracelets, chains, earrings, and other jewelry. He mentions the word "beauty" or "beautiful" at least three times in these passages. God had no problem with one adorning herself, because He adorned Israel. He said He placed that beauty on Israel (v. 14).

The problem came when Israel took God's blessing for granted and allowed itself to trust in its beauty and play the harlot.

But **thou didst trust in thine own beauty,** *and* **playedst the harlot** *because of thy renown, and* **pouredst out thy fornications** *on every one that passed by; his it was.*

Ezekiel 16:15

The adorning was never a problem with God or He would have never used those terms. Once again, the problem was the sin of the heart and how they used the beauty God had given them for seductive purposes.

And of thy garments thou didst take, and deckedst thy high places with divers colours, and playedst the harlot thereupon: the like things shall not come, neither shall it be so.

Thou hast also taken thy fair jewels of my gold and of my silver, which I had given thee, *and* **madest to thyself images of men, and didst commit whoredom with them** *. . . How weak is thine heart,* **saith the Lord** *God, seeing thou doest all these things, the work of an imperious whorish woman.*

Ezekiel 16:16-17,30

The problem was not the adornment. God said He gave it to them. It was how they used the things God gave them which was indicative of a weak heart. Everything goes back to the condition of the heart.

God's Validation of Makeup (Job's Daughter)

Most of us know the story of Job or have heard some kind of sermon about him and the tragedies that took place in his life. We know how he lost his livestock, cattle, and riches. We know that he was attacked with sickness in his body and all of his children were killed in a great storm.

In Chapter 42, God turned Job's captivity and blessed his latter end more than his beginning. He was blessed with seven sons and three daughters.

> *And he called the name of the first, Jemima; and the name of the second, Kezia;* **and the name of the third, Keren-happuch. And in all the land were no women found so fair as the daughters of Job:** *and their father gave them inheritance among their brethren.*
>
> Job 42:14-15

God blessed Job with daughters who were more fair or beautiful than any in all the land. Notice the name of Job's third daughter in verse 14: **Keren-happuch.** In Hebrew this name means **"horn of cosmetic,"** to paint the eyes with fair glistering colors.[1] In other words, she wore makeup.

Remember, God blessed Job with a daughter who wore makeup, whose very name meant "cosmetics." The man God called upright, who feared Him, turned away from evil, and was perfect in his heart toward God, had a daughter who exemplified beauty through the use of makeup. None in the land were more beautiful than Job's daughters.

God called all that was restored to Job blessed (v. 12). That means daughters who wore makeup were blessed. It

---

[1]James Strong. "Hebrew and Chaldee Dictionary," *The Exhaustive Concordance of the Bible* (Iowa Falls, IA: World Bible Publishers), p. 105, #7163 and p. 94, #6320.

also means that the people of God in biblical times wore makeup as an accepted form of beautification. There is no reprimand by God in this passage against Keren-happuch. Why? Because unlike the other women mentioned such as Jezebel, she had not opened her heart to idolatry or the spirits of whoredom and adultery as they had. This proves that the sin was never the makeup. It was a matter of the heart.

Adornment and the New Testament

> Also [I desire] that **women should adorn themselves modestly and appropriately** and sensibly in seemly apparel, not with [elaborate] hair arrangement or gold or pearls or expensive clothing, but by doing good deeds (deeds in themselves good and for the good and advantage of those contacted by them), as befits women who profess reverential fear for and devotion to God.
>
> 1 Timothy 2:9-10 AMP

> Likewise, ye wives, be in subjection to your own husbands; that, if any obey not the word, they also may without the word be won by the conversation of the wives; while they behold your chaste conversation coupled with fear.
>
> **Whose adorning let it not be that outward adorning of plaiting the hair, and of wearing of gold, or of putting on of apparel; but let it be the hidden man of the heart,** in that which is not corruptible, even the ornament of a meek and quiet spirit, which is in the sight of God of great price.
>
> 1 Peter 3:1-4

Jesus paid the price for us with His blood. He owns us and because He is our Lord, He has authority to regulate the way we live, act, and dress, as well as everything else that pertains to us.

In 1 Peter 3:3, Peter was not saying, "Don't plait the hair," or "Don't wear gold," because if that's the case, he had to be saying, "Don't put on any apparel or clothing either." We know God did not tell us not to wear any clothing. *The Amplified Version* of this scripture will help us to understand something:

> *Let not yours be the [merely] **external adorning** with [elaborate] interweaving and knotting of the hair, the wearing of jewelry, or changes of clothes.*

In other words, don't let your adornment be **merely** or just the outward adornment. Don't spend all your time on just fixing up outwardly. Don't spend all your time on dresses and clothes. God is not saying that a woman cannot dress up or fix herself up. He is saying, "Don't let the focus of your physical body become a higher priority over your spirit or inner man."

I believe if the Christian women who spend so much time in the mirror would give God half as much time in prayer and in the Word, they would be awesome spiritual giants. Peter is saying that women should dress the inward person with a meek and quiet spirit.

Women in ministry must definitely be careful to avoid extremes in their dress. When standing before people, if a woman's dress is too flashy or extravagant, it could cause people to be distracted from her message. She should lean to a more conservative approach and style of dress. I don't believe we have the right to lay down laws and commands. My job is not to regulate your conscience. Only you can do that. This is a matter between each woman and God.

The Pharisees who were students of the laws of Moses tried to interpret the law by the letter instead of by the Spirit. They placed unnecessary, unrequired demands and burdens upon the people of God. Many of the demands were never requirements made by God. Whenever we try to determine the interpretation of God's law by the letter, it always opens the door for additions to be made by man.

Even today, we see the same thing happening within various religious groups and denominations. In some churches earrings are allowed. In others they are not. Some allow extravagant hairstyles and others do not. Some wear hat coverings and others do not. Some are against "open-toe" shoes, yet others allow them.

Each individual must be led by the Holy Spirit. If wearing makeup violates a woman's conscience, she should not wear it. One cannot violate their own conscience and be at peace with God.

> *Hast thou faith? have it to thyself before God.* **Happy is he that condemneth not himself in that thing which he alloweth.** *And* **he that doubteth is damned if he eat,** *because he eateth not of faith:* **for whatsoever is not of faith is sin.**
>
> Romans 14:22-23

Our purpose is not to get every woman to start wearing makeup. We are only trying to bring *balance* to erroneous, condemning, traditional teaching that has taught that all adorning and makeup is sin. If you cannot wear makeup in good conscience, without doubting and believing that it is the will of God for you to wear it, then you are in sin.

I knew of a lady who was a member of our church who came from a strict church when it came to makeup, adorning, and wearing slacks. No matter how free the women of our church were, when it came to wearing makeup, she just could not do it. It had been pounded in her for so long that it was a sinful act. She tried wearing it for a while just to identify with the other women of the church. However, she could not continue because her conscience was not at peace.

It had to be one of two problems: 1) Either she had a lack of knowledge of God's Word, or 2) God, for whatever reason, did not want her to wear makeup. You might ask, "How would God biblically allow it, but not allow it for her as an individual?" God deals with all of us individually, based upon our hearts or what is best for us. For example, going to a shopping mall is not a sin. However, if you have a weakness shopping and overspending, God may direct you not to shop for a while in order for you to get control of that problem.

It could have been that this young lady at one time had a seductive spirit surrounding the use of makeup. She could have possibly used the makeup as a dependence for being accepted by people or getting attention and God saw the need to break her from this subtle form of idolatry. Yet, for others this may not be the case. As I stated, God deals with each of us differently.

My wife came from a very strict Pentecostal Holiness church background. Although she wore slacks and makeup during her adult years, she respected her family's home and church. She would not allow her liberty to offend them. She would not wear the makeup when she went around them.

It took her some time before she developed true peace when wearing it. After she got a revelation of God's Word and saw that God did not condemn makeup and slacks, her conscience was finally free to wear them in peace. She no longer had doubts, but she had faith that it was the will of God. (I will discuss the "slacks" issue in the next chapter.)

The battle over how to dress goes back to the age-old battle that dictates how we live our lives in every area: *the flesh vs. the Spirit* (Galatians 5:16-18). If women allow themselves to be led by the Spirit, they will know how to dress. The Spirit within them will guide them into that which is pleasing to God. When a woman is carnal or motivated by the flesh, her dress will seek to draw attention to self rather than to glorify Christ.

I teach women that they should dress up and look nice for themselves and their husbands within the confines of what Christ requires. Allow me to give you some general principles you can use to help guide you in this matter.

1. Make sure that your adornment is not seductive. Hairstyles, makeup, jewelry, and clothing will be seductive if that is what is in the heart (Proverbs 12:26; Mark 7:21; Revelation 2:20). If you are not for sale, take your sign down!

2. Do not allow your adornment to cause those of the opposite sex to stumble. Make sure when you are looking in the mirror to dress and groom yourself for the day, you are not trying to accentuate your sexuality and causing men to lust (Romans 14:13; Proverbs 6:25).

3. Do not try to accentuate private body parts. Cleavages should be fully covered and clothing around the hips and buttocks should fit loosely and appropriately. Also be conscious of dress length.

4. Always demonstrate moderation (Philippians 4:5). That means to be mild, gentle, appropriate; not extravagant, flamboyant, or sensuous.

5. Your body should glorify God (1 Corinthians 6:20). Keep in mind that no matter where we go, we represent Christ. Do not let your witness for Christ be tarnished. The way a person dresses indicates a lot about their personality or who they are as an individual.

6. If you are married, seek to please your husband in your dress and adornment (1 Corinthians 7:34; Amos 3:3).

19

Is It a Sin for a Woman To Wear Slacks?

*The woman shall not wear that which pertaineth unto a man, neither shall a man put on a woman's garment: for all that do so are **abomination** unto the Lord thy God.*
Deuteronomy 22:5

This is the only scripture in the Bible that anti-slacks wearing proponents can use to defend their position. Since pants (or slacks) are what the man wears, they say a woman should not wear them.

It's amazing how the woman's blouse or shirt was never attacked because it's similar to the shirt that a man wears. Just as the pants is a garment that pertains to a man, so is the shirt. Keep in mind the scripture in Deuteronomy never specified which garment. It never specified pants (slacks) or shirts. Therefore, if we are going to interpret this scripture in light of how anti-pants groups have interpreted it, then women wearing shirts or blouses is a sin because it pertains to a man's garment.

Please allow me to use my imagination here. I believe some preacher many, many years ago saw a woman in pants. It may have shown her figure a little more than what he or she could handle. Because of their distorted views of sex and sexuality, they saw it as seductive clothing and made a doctrine out of it. I will admit that a woman can wear pants (or slacks) clad too tightly to her body. Christian women, especially women ministers, must be very careful of this. However, that still does not mean that women wearing pants as a whole is a sin.

The real issue is, what is culturally acceptable? What does the culture view as acceptable clothing for females, and yet they are still looked upon as being a female or feminine? Our American culture permits women to wear pants (slacks) made for females. This does not mean that they are trying to look like men. In Scotland, it is culturally acceptable for the men to wear kilts, which resemble a woman's skirt. This has been a part of their culture for centuries now. For a man to wear a skirt in the United States, however, would be totally unacceptable. People would immediately think he is a "cross dresser." A woman in pants (or slacks) does not bring that kind of reaction because it is an accepted fashion for a woman in our country.

In biblical days, Jewish clothing worn by women was practically the same as the men. Women wore the same five basic garments as the men. Veils were probably the greatest difference. Women wore cloaks and robes as well as the men. As a matter of fact, the undergarments that women wore were similar to pants.

The bottom line is, when a woman is wearing a man's clothing, is she trying to look or act like a man? When a man is wearing a woman's clothing, is he trying to look or act like a woman? Some homosexuals like to put on women's clothes or vice versa. They like to impersonate women. Today we call them transvestites and/or cross dressers. This was the real problem. This scripture had to mean something deeper of the heart than just the simple act of a woman wearing some pants.

> *Thou shalt not lie with mankind, as with womankind:*
> *it is **abomination**.*
>
> Leviticus 18:22

God is dealing with homosexuality here. The key word in this passage is "abomination." It is the same word God uses in Deuteronomy 22:5 pertaining to women wearing men's garments. Once again, *this is an issue of the heart.*

A former minister from my church was once in a very strict Pentecostal Holiness denomination that taught against women wearing pants (or slacks). His mind was not free to accept it until he went to a conference where women were falling under the power of God and speaking in tongues while wearing pants. He even saw women in ministry wearing pants (slacks) ministering under the power of God to other women. He recognized God's power and came to the conclusion that God would not anoint anything that He was against. His view of women in slacks has been different ever since.

Only tradition has said that women should not wear pants. The Bible has never said anything to that effect. Here is the balance. If you are working with or ministering to a group of people who have an anti view of women wearing slacks, makeup, or anything pertaining to dress and adornment, you would do well to conform to their dress standards so that you will not be a stumbling block to them. Love will not allow your liberty to be a stumbling block to others. You should not go into a place trying to sway people over to your beliefs just because it's not the way you believe.

Notice how Paul instructed us to handle those "gray area" issues that we sometimes disagree on. In his day, eating various meats or esteeming certain days were the hot issues that Christians did not agree on. Let's do a little reading exercise. Replace the words "meat" and "esteeming days" with "pants" and "makeup." (This is for illustration only. I am in no way changing the Word of God.)

Wherefore, if meat [pants] **make my brother to offend,** *I will eat no flesh* [wear no pants] *while the world standeth, lest I make my brother to offend.*
1 Corinthians 8:13

For one believeth that he may eat all things [wear pants]: another, who is weak, eateth herbs [does not wear pants].

Let not him that eateth [wear pants] despise him that eateth not [does not wear pants]; and let not him which eateth not [does not wear pants] judge him that eateth [wear pants]: for God hath received him . . .

One man esteemeth one day [esteems makeup] above another: another esteemeth every day [no makeup] alike. Let every man [woman] be fully persuaded in his [her] own mind.

He that regardeth the day [use of makeup], regardeth it unto the Lord; and he that regardeth not the day [no makeup], to the Lord he doth not regard it. He that eateth, eateth to the Lord, for he giveth God thanks; and he that eateth not, to the Lord he eateth not, and giveth God thanks . . .

Let us not therefore judge one another any more: but judge this rather, that no man put a stumblingblock or an occasion to fall in his brother's way.

Romans 14:2-3,5-6,13

But take heed lest by any means this liberty of yours become a stumblingblock to them that are weak.

1 Corinthians 8:9

If you are in a church that demands no makeup or pants (slacks) and you feel that you cannot conform, rather than be a stumbling block to others, you should pray about moving on to a church that shares your beliefs.

Conclusion

In conclusion, I pray that this book will bring clarity to your heart and mind concerning these various women's issues. It is not intended to be used to attack pastors. Do not demand changes. Do not try to rally support and organize others to take over the church. Share this book or what you have learned with him. If your pastor is not willing to change and you are not willing to conform, you may want to pray about leaving rather than causing discord (Proverbs 6:19). Just because you have these truths now does not mean everyone will see it or accept it.

Even though God permitted the eating of meats (1 Corinthians 8:4-8), some, because of conscience or lack of knowledge, could not eat the meat used for the worship of idols. Some people will close their minds to certain truths and not want to believe anything contrary to what they already believe. Yet God leaves it to every man to be persuaded in his own heart and allow God to judge in the end (Romans 14:5,10).

A person who believes that Saturday is the day of worship to God should go to a church that believes in Saturday worship rather than try to change a whole church to their theological beliefs.

If you believe that a woman should preach, teach, lead, not wear head coverings, makeup, or slacks, rather than fight and cause discord, move on. God will judge that leader for his error. But He will also judge you for your rebellion. Jesus did not try to stay in a church that did not want to receive the truth that He had to offer. After they put Him out of the synagogue, He did not stay and try to fight or rally other sympathizing members to His side. Instead, He moved on (Luke 4:16-30).

Bibliography

Coleman, William L. *Today's Handbook of Bible Times and Customs*. Minneapolis, MN: Bethany House Publishing.

Coner, Kevin. *The Church in the New Testament*. Portland, OR: Bible Temple Publishing.

Eberle, Harold. *The Living Sword*. Yakima, WA: Winepress Ministries.

Hagin, Kenneth E. *The Woman Question*. Tulsa, OK: Kenneth Hagin Ministries.

Smith, Dr. J. L. and Dr. S. A. Moore. *Why Trouble Ye the Women?* Columbus, GA: Brentwood Christian Press.